Samuel Cockburn

The Laws of Nature and the Laws of God

A Reply to Prof. Drummond

Samuel Cockburn

The Laws of Nature and the Laws of God
A Reply to Prof. Drummond

ISBN/EAN: 9783744754361

Printed in Europe, USA, Canada, Australia, Japan

Cover: Foto ©ninafisch / pixelio.de

More available books at **www.hansebooks.com**

THE LAWS OF NATURE AND
THE LAWS OF GOD.

THE LAWS OF NATURE

AND

THE LAWS OF GOD:

A REPLY TO PROF. DRUMMOND

BY

SAMUEL COCKBURN, M.D., L.R.C.S.E

LONDON:
SWAN SONNENSCHEIN, LE BAS & LOWREY.
PATERNOSTER SQUARE.
1886.

PREFACE.

Though conscious of many literary defects in this Reply, I have a hope that it may to some extent, however limited, neutralise the baneful effects resulting from the attempt now being made in different quarters to square the teachings of revealed religion with the uncertain findings and ever changing speculations of modern science and philosophy.

Science and religion belong to two entirely different spheres. Each is cultivated and advanced by its own special modes and principles; and each is subject to its own special tests. The one is entirely independent of the other, and they ought never to be pitted the one against the other, nor brought into collision. Let the motto in each sphere be— Truth, as we see it; Truth, as we know it; Truth, whithersoever it leads.

The attempt to harmonise science and religion is uncalled for, and totally unnecessary. Science with all its brilliant past and still more brilliant future may be safely left to itself, and its many earnest cultivators are perfectly able to look after themselves. Religion with all its past victories and brilliant achievements in the social, moral, and spiritual culture of the race, and its still more glorious and transcendant future, needs no props, and no patronising support either from science or philosophy, and its many

Preface. iii

representatives are perfectly able to defend themselves.

The natural laws of the material universe will ever form a rich field for the exercise of man's natural reason and ingenuity, and each worker will be rewarded according to the lines on which he works, and the ability and perseverance with which he conducts that work. But the laws which hold good in the spiritual sphere of a man's being, and in that world where lies his future home, are not the product of man's reason and ingenuity. They must be revealed *to* him, and he becomes their recipient only according to his individual moral state, and not in virtue of his scientific or philosophical attainments.

The scope and sphere of the natural laws are in the seen and temporal. The scope and sphere of the spiritual laws are in the unseen and the eternal. Professor Drummond wishes to teach that the laws of the one sphere are not different and distinct from the laws of the other, but that they are one and the same. And seeing that the natural laws as discovered by man are at best only tentative and approximative, not absolutely true and final, it would be very sad indeed if the laws which hold good in the spiritual sphere were always to be changed and modified according to the opinions and ideas which might happen to prevail at any particular time regarding such natural laws. It would also be equally sad if the great bulk of Christian men and women who are neither skilled in science nor versed in philosophy were obliged to go to men, many of whom neither believe in a God nor a future life, and receive from them the guide to, and the guarantee of the laws which hold good in the spiritual sphere!

As a whole, I cannot look upon Drummond's book as in any sense an attempt to discover the fixed laws of Nature, and to trace these into the spiritual sphere, which would have been a most interesting and profitable inquiry, but rather as a natural effort to support and perpetuate certain aspects of a sectarian theology on the ground that he could prove that theology to be in perfect accord with modern science and philosophy. And while it is right that every mode, every process, and every part in nature ought as far as possible to be made subservient to the teaching and illustration of spiritual truths, Christ himself having largely done so, I should strongly suspect and fear any system of theology which in any degree depended upon, or that in its essentials was in perfect harmony with, the laws of modern science and philosophy.

Sir D. Brewster was an eminent man of science, and a genuine Christian. Faraday was also a prominent leader in scientific research, and at the same time a man of well-pronounced Christian character. These and many others have been earnest cultivators of science, and at the same time genuine Christians, making no effort to reconcile or harmonise their religious belief with their scientific studies. Why should the wants and the longings of the immortal soul be checked or imperilled by considerations of science and philosophy? They required no Huxley and no Darwin to explain to them the laws of spiritual life. And they felt no want of a Herbert Spencer to unfold or gaurantee to them the truthfulness of Christ's doctrine of eternal life, or spiritual Death. They acknowledged one guide, and only one authority, God's word, the sure word of prophecy; and that one guide and one authority will be ours. The Christian religion can never be injured by any attack from an external enemy; but it is, and it always has been, in danger of being seriously injured by professed friends in their endeavour to incorporate into its doctrines the teachings of philosophy falsely so called!

SAMUEL COCKBURN, M.D.

172 BATH ST., GLASGOW
January, 1886.

# REPLY TO DRUMMOND.

CHAPTER I.

BEFORE entering on a review of Professor Drummond's work entitled "Natural Law in the Spiritual World," we must first give expression to our high appreciation of the many excellencies in that book. It is written in a most fascinating and charming style, and it manifests all through a thoroughly Christian spirit. It shows that the author has a very complete knowledge of the achievements of modern science; that he is also thoroughly versed in all the theoretical sociology and speculative philosophy of the present day, that he is well versed in the Holy Scriptures, and knows well how to use these in the defence and support of his theories. We cannot, however, conceal the conviction that his faith in, and attachment to, modern speculative science and philosophy is much too strong and wholly unwarranted. The history of the past shows that every form of science and philosophy has been advanced only to be demolished in turn by new experiments and more recent speculations, and there is no reason to expect that the one or the other in our day will prove any exception to their predecessors. Finality and perfection have not yet been reached. And further, it is all but universally conceded that the science and philosophy of the present day are more directly opposed to the teachings and truths of revealed religion than any which have been advanced for half a century before, and that on that account they require to be looked at very carefully and guardedly. No one knows this better than Professor Drummond, and it is perfectly possible that his attachment to modern science and philosophy may be more apparent than real, and that the doctrines of modern biology, evolution, and sociology have been adopted because they offer specially suitable media for the dissemination of doctrines which, if more plainly pronounced and in the ordinary language of men, might be rather unsavoury. In this view of the case he has been most successful.

It will be quite impossible in the compass of a short review to look at the preface and introduction—two most important parts of the work; nor yet will it be possible to take up *all* the questionable statements contained in the various chapters; we must restrict ourselves to the most prominent features of the work.

The first chapter is entitled Biogenises, which treats of the origin of life. The Professor says "there is no life without life." There can be no life without antecedent life. And on this foundation he raises a very strange superstructure. The statement apparently means a great deal, but in reality it adds nothing whatever to the doctrine universally taught and universally accepted all over Christendom. In the Bible we are taught that God is the Source and Origin of all life. And about this there can be no mistake, for there is no ambiguity about the language. But the scientific standpoint of "no life without previous life" is rather a slippery foundation to build upon.

In the grand old Book we have what may be called a condensed summary of the creation of all things. This account starts with God as the Creator, and traces the gradual development of creative work from the lowest forms of existence up to man, who is the highest manifestation of creative skill and power—a being made in the image and likeness of his great Creator. And it certainly would have been more in keeping with the spiritual culture of the age had Professor Drummond started his inquiry from this basis. But simply to say that there is no life without previous life, is, as we will find, a very ambiguous statement. Conventionally speaking, it is acknowledged that all *forms* of life imply the existence of previous life. But scientifically speaking, it has no claim to be looked upon as a universal truth. If by the statement that there is no life without previous life is meant that all life now existing has been produced from, or created by, previous life, we must dissent from the statement; life is never created or produced. It is uncreatable. And yet the statement is capable of covering this.

The scientific doctrine of Biogenises with its associated doctrine of evolution is intended to dispense with the existence of God as a creator altogether. Life in no form can be produced or created, for God *only* is life, and has life in Himself, and from Him *alone* all and every degree of life comes. Modern scientists, in place of starting their investigations from the one great First Cause, start from man and pursue their investigations backwards, till they come, not to God, but to a glutinous kind of matter which they call protoplasm, as the beginning of all living creatures, and to the mineral which they say is dead. This is all the scientist can give us as the goal of his inquiries. And strange, these positions are essential to the doctrines which Professor Drummond wishes to inculcate.

He refers to the three great divisions of nature, namely, the animal, the vegetable, and the mineral, and shows that the mineral has no power to become a plant, and that the plant has no power to become an animal; that if ever the mineral is to become a plant, the plant must act upon it and mould it into part of its own structure. And so if the plant is ever to· become an animal the animal must act upon it and incorporate it into part of its own organisation. And that exactly the same thing holds good in the spiritual sphere.

Now the doctrine he wishes to enforce from this is, that a natural man is just as dead spiritually as a crystal—that there is no possibility whatever of a natural man becoming spiritually minded unless some outside power acts upon him in the same way that the plant does upon the mineral, or the animal does upon the plant. We hold that there is no analogy between the two, much less identity. In support and elucidation of his position, he introduces the case of Biogenises *versus* spontaneous generation; but here we think he either misapprehends or misrepresents what is essential in the doctrine of spontaneous generation. He says "a thousand modern pulpits are every day preaching the doctrine of spontaneous generation." But by spontaneous generation he means that something which is virtually and absolutely dead can of its own accord become living. Now that is perfectly absurd. No one believes anything of the kind. About life in the abstract we know nothing. Life is omnipresent as God is. Where He is there is life. Life in some form exists everywhere. The forms of life are infinite and everchanging. These forms are determined by surrounding conditions and circumstances, the active agent being their inherent power or force of life, call it what you will, given by God Himself. We can predicate of life only from its manifestations. The chemist cannot precipitate it; the scientist cannot give it a form.

The philosopher in his highest flights cannot catch it. It is everywhere where God is. The chemist can measure and weigh the nitrogen and the oxygen in the atmosphere; but neither oxygen nor nitrogen are life. And yet the atmosphere is full of life. From the food we eat and the water we drink we build up and maintain the structure of our bodies—the house we live in; but as at the beginning, so now, to a large extent we derive life from the atmosphere through our nostrils.

The forms of matter are often determined by conditions under the control of man, and thus in so far as the forms are concerned he becomes a creator in the sense of a potter; he creates nothing from himself as God does; but the clay and the life being there, he can determine forms. This marvellous power he has hitherto—consciously or otherwise—exercised to his shame and loss. There are noxious and destructive forms of matter which in a paradisaical condition could have had no existence, and which never were created by God, and which in a truly regenerated condition could be of no use, and consequently could not exist. We need only mention in this connection all the family of parasites and the widespread, destructive germs of disease. Who can doubt that there are a vast number of organisms of a destructive character directly the product of diverted and perverted forces? This, no doubt, opens up a very wide subject which we cannot further enter on here. But what we mean is this, that, while God alone is the Creator, man has also a creative power in his own finite degree in so far as he can corrupt and pervert the Divine order of things, and thereby bring into existence a vast multitude of evil active forms which otherwise would never have had any existence.

Given the material, and given the perverted conditions and circumstances and you have the perverted product. That is all that is essential in the doctrine of spontaneous generation. God did not create the product—man did it—in direct opposition to the Divine order of things. The doctrine of the scientists on whom the professor relies is this, that every existing organism, no matter what it is—a mite or a maggot, a monkey or a man—is the direct offspring of a previous maggot, monkey or man, back *ad infinitum*, or as some of them believe that man is merely the product of the natural law of evolution, that at one time he was a monkey, and further back, only a mite or a maggot, and further back still, a mere globule of glutinous matter dignified with the high sounding phrase, *protoplasm*.

We now come to the spiritual aspect of the subject. The professor holds and repeats over and over again that there is the same difference between a natural man and a spiritual man that there is between the mineral and the plant. On this doctrine he bestows a large amount of skilful argument. It is his fundamental argument. If this is wrong, all his scientific theories go for nothing. And here, we consider, lies his fundamental error.

The Bible doctrine of spiritual death he completely misrepresents. Science is of no use here. It is a Bible phrase, a

Bible fact, and a Bible doctrine, and must be settled on Bible testimony and evidence. An appeal to plants and minerals is outside the subject. A natural man is not as dead as a crystal. Spiritual death has no meaning of this kind. Spiritual death essentially implies that the spiritual part of the man is still existing and active, but perverted and depraved. Directed to selfishness and sensuality, devoted to the service of the devil, the world and the flesh, and consequently actually dead as regards the love and the service of God. A crystal is just what God made it. Very good. A Spiritually dead man is not as God made him. And in place of being very good he is corrupted and very bad. A crystal is not responsible for being what it is, but a spiritually dead man is responsible for being what he is. He is in no sense like the passive crystal when the active living plant seizes hold of it and moulds it into part of its own living structure. Nor like the plant when the animal seizes hold of it and incorporates it into its own living organism. Nothing of the kind, but the very reverse. And yet we are asked to believe that the law and the relationship are the same in both. In place of that, the spiritually dead man is in arms against God. He is a rebel. He is not passive in any sense. He is the prodigal son—voluntarily leaving his fathers home—voluntarily spending his substance in riotous living. Not dead like the crystal in any sense, but alive to sin though dead to God and goodness.

During conversion or regeneration, we have the very same activity, not dead and passive like the crystal. The prodigal thinks—thinks seriously—comes to himself—yes, to himself; his relationship of sonship to a Father in Heaven. Not that he was merely a higher kind of animal. Not dead like a crystal. But a son wandered from his heavenly home. And realising this he determines to give up his riotous living and return to his Father and with all humility and penitence, yet with earnestness and alacrity he returns to his Father.

The professor teaches that man is merely a higher kind of animal. His words are these—" He is endowed simply with a higher quality of the animal life." We dissent from this. Man is a distinct, separate and higher creature altogether than any kind of animal. Man has a dual nature. However debased and degraded, he has besides his merely animal organisation a spiritual nature which is never lost, here nor hereafter. Logically speaking, it is incorrect to predicate death or deadness of a crystal. Inertia is a property of matter, not death. Death can only be predicated of something which *has* been living. All through this chapter he looks upon man as merely a higher kind of animal. He ignores or denies that man has a spiritual nature quite distinct from the animal. A spiritual nature by which he can consciously be in communion with and realise the presence of God. A nature which can understand and receive spiritual truth, and under the influence of which he can again become God-like.

The scientists whom the professor takes as his authorities in natural law do not acknowledge God as the creator of man or the universe. God is ousted from the world he has made, and something called Force associated with matter put in His place. In a spiritual point of view this is destructive to all just inquiry. God is not only the creator of the universe, but he is the maintainer and constant sustainer of all that he created. Nothing has an independent life in, or of, itself. The life of all and each is continuously from God. God does not measure out a certain quantity of life to each and go away and leave it. Life comes continuously from Him. He alone is life. This is not only true of plants and animals, but of minerals as well. The integrity of these latter—their very existence depends upon what scientists call, not by the name of life, but by the term forces, namely, chemical affinity, cohesion, gravity. But these forces are not self-existing—not self-created—

they are from God, and are in reality only another name for life. The professor says they are dead, but all scientists say they contain or embody forces, and the word force is only another name for life. All that God created is filled with life according to the ends and uses it was intended to serve.

In proving his argument about the natural man being dead, the Professor takes advantage of mere verbal expressions without any due consideration or reference to their intrinsic meaning. Thus, "he that hath the Son hath life:" "he that hath not the Son hath not life;" and from this he assumes that Christ as a person enters into the man. Now there are two fallacies here. Seeing that he does not recognise the existence naturally in any human being of a spiritual nature, it follows that, if Christ is to enter and dwell in the man, it must be that he enters into the natural man, or what he calls the merely higher animal, and dwells there. Who can believe this? The merely animal part of our nature continues even in the regenerated man an animal nature still. The animal nature is never converted for the simple reason that the animal nature was not the transgressor. The first condition imposed upon Adam and that still applies to all his descendants was this—"the soul that sinneth it shall die"—not the animal nature that sinneth. It is the spiritual, the soul part of the man that is converted and regenerated, and through that the merely higher animal part is to be guided, governed, and kept in its proper place.

At page 74 he says, "Life depends upon

contact with life." This, in the natural plane, is true, but it does not fairly represent the spiritual truth. Spiritual life involves quality besides mere life. A man might be in contact with life, true life, and yet he himself be practically a dead man. Man has the power of perverting what he receives from God. The life-giving power of the natural sun, as it falls on the mass of decomposing matter, is the same which falls on the rose or the sweet violet, but how different are the results. From the one we have hateful odours and destructive malaria; from the other delightful and refreshing fragrance. The life is the same in both—the source the same. But how different the outcome! The recipient must be changed —not the life. And then he refers to Nicodemus in support of this theory.

But the fact is, Nicodemus's case is dead against the theory. Christ's reply to the ruler was, not that he should get into contact with life, but that he, the man himself, must be changed. "Ye must be born again." Nicodemus was a very learned man, but his learning, no matter how correct and varied, was of no use to him here. Neither he then, nor can any scientific man now, by his scientific learning understand how a man when he was old could be born again. It was a biological puzzle to Nicodemus then, as it is a "biological conceit" to scientists now. But there is no help for it. He, the man Nicodemus, must be born again before he could enter the kingdom of Heaven. Not that the mere corporeal body, the higher animal, was to be born again—that was impossible—but the conscious, rational, thinking man dwelling within that body, that was to be born again. The change was an interior one, and such as is often referred to as a change of heart.

In further proof of the assertion that Christ personally enters into the man, he gives the case of Paul, who was converted when on his way to Damascus. But here, too, Christ did not in any sense enter into Paul, but His word did—the truth did. And that truth was like a two-edged sword. Divine truth is the voice, the word of God, and that convicts, converts, and saves.

It is no valid objection to say that God must be present to convict and convert; God is always present. He leaves no one, no, not for an instant. But for the presence, the life-giving and life-sustaining presence of God, no one could continue to exist. In the lowest conditions of ignorance, depravity, and degradation, God is ever with His creatures, with them for their good. But while this is so, we have all naturally false and perverted ideas about God and divine things, and until the truth as it is revealed and embodied in Christ comes home to us, we are dead to God and all that is Godlike. But when the truth does come home to us, the man becomes a new man. The persecuting Saul of Tarsus becomes Paul the living apostle; and men are condemned not because Christ does not come into them, but because they voluntarily and persistently resist the truth which the Spirit of God is ever using to convert and save them. Besides stifling and rejecting these more personal and interior strivings and drawings of the Spirit, which every man in the secret of his own soul has at some time or other been conscious of, Christ dwells in the Christian in the same way as the Christian dwells in Christ—not personally. Christ dwells in the Christian when His truth dwells in the heart and changes that heart into His own glorious image, making him Christlike, and in no other way.

The two points this chapter was intended to establish — namely, that a natural man as regards all spiritual life is as dead as a crystal, and that man is merely a higher kind of animal, it has entirely failed to do.

Speak to a crystal or a plant, a monkey or an elephant, on any spiritual subject, and you may try till doomsday, but you will get no response. Speak to any of the higher animals of God of a future life, of a judgment day, of heaven, and what response will you get? None! No, man is essentially a different being altogether from any other creature; he is a spiritual being, and by virtue of that he can apprehend and understand something about a spiritual world, and something about spiritual truths; he is an immortal being, and by virtue of that he can apprehend and understand something about an immortal life beyond the grave. No crystal, no plant, no mere higher animal can do this. This immortal soul is degraded and depraved to a terrible degree; but it is still there. The image of God can never be entirely lost or effaced; and to that depraved soul God in His word is ever making the appeal, 'Awake thou that sleepest, arise from the dead, and Christ shall give thee light."

EPITOME.

The law of Biogenises in the natural sphere is directly opposed to the law of Biogenises in the spiritual sphere in the following three essentials :

First. The crystal is just what God made it and intended it to be. In direct opposition to this, the man spiritually dead is not what God made him, and not what God intended him to be.

Second. The crystal is not conscious of any want of any kind. In opposition to this, the dead soul, even according to Drummond, misses God, longs, yearns, and pines for God. This is very unlike the crystal.

Third. The crystal receives no life

whatever from the plant. In place of that, the plant cannot live without the crystal; its very existence depends upon it. In opposition to this, the dead soul does receive life from God, and depends entirely upon God for its very existence.

CHAPTER II.

DEGENERATION.

This chapter undoubtedly contains some highly instructive lessons. Its tendency, however, if not its legitimate outcome, is to support the doctrine of the final annihilation of the unsaved.

The natural law the professor wishes to carry into the spiritual sphere is simply this—that organs which are not exercised gradually waste away, and ultimately become extinct; and this in the spiritual sphere means, that if the soul's salvation is neglected, it will also shrivel and shrink, till it is lost altogether. Now at the outset here, we have the same fallacy we had in the former chapter, and when this is clearly seen, the fallacy all through will be easily detected. The mere fact that a person utterly and entirely neglects his soul's salvation, is no reason nor proof that his soul will shrink and waste away. Nothing of the kind. In place of that, by neglecting the soul's salvation, the soul itself may be developing into fiendish proportions. He ignores all through the fact that the unregenerated man is constantly exercising his soul. As to its wasting away and becoming smaller is nonsense. Size, as applied to a soul, has no rational meaning. The soul is determined by quality, not size. As an illustration of the natural law in the case he gives as instances the mole, and certain subterranean fishes, which have entirely lost their eyes by neglecting to use them. If the same thing takes place in the afterlife with the soul because it has not been exercised, then the person must cease to exist. We see no way of escaping this conclusion, and we know that many who have carefully read this chapter have been led to conclude that it either supports or is intended to teach the doctrine of the annihilation of the unsaved.

As another illustration of the process of degeneracy leading to the final catastrophe, he gives the case of a man who is seen to fall from a five-storey building. The moment we see him fall we say he is lost—lost before he gets to the ground. And the same he holds is true in regard to a natural man; whether he knows it or not, he is lost. Now, here the cases are not at all analogous. In the case of the man falling from the house-top, the moment he begins to fall, his death is certain—the final result is inevitable. The man is lost, and more than that, cannot be again restored to life. In the spiritual realm this is not the case. Neither is there anything like it. Though immediately on the first transgression man fell, and thereby became essentially spiritually dead, the final result was not inevitable. It was not inevitable in the case of the first man—neither is it inevitable in the case of any man who is within the sound of the Gospel message. The first man we have no doubt was caught in his falling, and saved, and is now alive in glory. And thank God a multitude that no man can number—many of whom had fallen low, very low—have been caught in their downward course and are now amongst the saved, trophies of redeeming grace. The Gospel call to *all* is not simply and only a call. It is a call based upon and involving a fact that there is salvation within the reach of, and intended for, all. The law in the natural world does not hold good in the spiritual; for the falling man in the spiritual sphere may be stopped in his fall, and may live and not die.

Further on he says, "By the sheer action of a natural law," a man sinks into hell. This is a harsh statement, and entirely untrue. A man may sink into hell *according* to a natural law; but no man will ever sink into hell *by* the sheer action of a natural law. In the one case, the man is his own destroyer; in the other, he is the unfortunate victim of the action of a natural law, which is a very different thing.

That man is fallen, depraved and corrupted, is certain, universally so, certain, but the way in which the doctrine is put by Drummond is erroneous and very misleading. He simply substantiates the doctrine of the materialist which says that man is the creature of his organization, and consequently, not responsible for what he does.

We hold that man is not the creature of his organization, and that he does not sin by virtue of any innate law of his being to do so, but just the very reverse. We hold that the man is the head and the superior over all his faculties and members, and that it is the will of God that the man should make all the powers of his being subservient to the service and glory of his Creator, and that God has fitted and adapted him for this, and given him all the means of doing it.

Were this not the case no man could ever blame himself for doing what was wrong. It is this adaptation and fitness to do what is right which lies at the foundation of the very idea of wrong. Without this there could be no individual responsibility.

In the same chapter he says—" We are apt to imagine that nature is full of life; in reality it is full of death. One cannot say it is natural for a plant to live. Air is not life, but corruption; so literally corruption that the only way to keep out corruption when life has closed is to keep out air." Nature, we hold, is *full* of life, notwithstanding this deliverance—full of it. Indeed, as a substantive existence there is no such thing as Death. We should like to see any one try to prove its existence.

We often speak of death; but we

mean thereby merely the qualitative state of deadness or the absence of all vital phenomena—never of it as an entity. With life it is quite different. God is everywhere and in everything, and God is essentially life. The change which comes over plants and animals which we call death is a mere change in form.

The substance enters into new forms, and manifests life in these new forms.

Air is an essential to all and every form of life both in plants and animals. The exclusion of air at once arrests that life, and the exclusion of air from a plant which has produced its seed and served its purpose, does not preserve that plant from death, as is alleged; but in reality prevents the plant from entering into new and more extended forms of life. Every one knows this. Take the seed of any plant or fruit, and seal it up from the action of the air, and it remains in a state of deadness. But put the same seed into the ground, supply it with air and moisture, and it soon springs up into new and varied forms of life. Life is everywhere.

At page 108, the spiritual cure for degeneracy, he says, is—"To take resolute hold of the upward power, and be brought by it to the upward goal." This may be scientific language, but it is scarcely scriptural. With all due deference to the solemnity of the subject, it forcibly reminds one of the idea of being taken u to heaven in a balloon.

On to the end of the chapter he confounds the truth which saves with the organ or power which apprehends or takes hold of the truth; and draws the conclusion that as moles and certain fish have neglected to use their eyes, nature has avenged herself by taking away the eyes altogether. And so in the same way will men, who have neglected the great salvation, lose their souls. As an illustration of this he gives the case of the man with the one talent. But in place of supporting the theory, this case exposes its fallacy. Though a man neglects the great salvation, God never takes his soul away, nor destroys it in any sense whatever, as nature takes away the eyes of the moles or fishes. The one talent given to the man was such a form of truth or knowledge, which, if honestly and faithfully applied to practical life, would have ennobled the man, and glorified his God; but by rolling it in a napkin and burying it, it was abused and rendered useless. And at last it, the talent, was taken away from him altogether. And so at last will it be with every one. Whatever knowledge a man may possess here of the way of life, of the Will of God, of the great salvation, if that has been rolled in a napkin and buried, in place of being used for the purification and sanctification of the whole man and also for the good of others—all such knowledge will be taken away from him altogether. God did not take away the soul from the man who had abused his one talent. That soul, though degenerating, was not wasting away, but was growing in worldliness, meanness and selfishness.

EPITOME.

The Law of Degeneracy in the natural sphere is opposed to the Law of Degeneracy in the spiritual sphere in the three following particulars:

First. In the natural sphere, the unused organ shrinks and shrivels. Whereas, in the spiritual sphere, the spiritual organs are never unused, and never shrink nor shrivel.

Second. In the natural sphere, an unused organ becomes feeble and decays. Whereas, in the spiritual sphere, a soul not used in the service of God may be growing and developing into terrible forms of moral and spiritual depravity.

Third. In the natural sphere an unused organ ultimately disappears altogether. In the spiritual sphere, the soul, though lost to God and all that is good, is never taken away. If the soul is to be taken away, like the unused organ, then annihilation is the doctrine.

CHAPTER III.

GROWTH.

This is a charming chapter to read. It is so simple, so natural like. In its details of modes and processes it is most instructive, but in principle, we think, it is wrong. " Consider the lilies how they grow, they toil not, they spin not; and yet Solomon in all his glory was not arrayed like one of these."

The general idea throughout is simply this, that as the lilies neither toil nor spin, yet they grow; therefore a Christian should not strive nor make any special effort to grow in grace, God will do it all for him. The lilies grow automatically and spontaneously; so should the Christian grow in grace, without trying to do so. Such is the line of teaching. The principle involved in this, we think, is wrong—there is no analogy between the growth of a soul in grace and the growth of a plant. A cabbage or a turnip grow without any effort; that is true, but, not only so, they have no control whatever over their growth. Surely no one can imagine that a Christian man can grow in grace, and make no more effort to do so than the cabbage does? No one can say that a Christian man has no control for or against his growth in grace. Plants grow naturally and in order with no effort. A man's body grows in the same way, and for the same reason. They are devoid of volition—plants grow without volition, spontaneously—no Christian can grow without volition and determination.

The growth of a plant and the growth of a soul in grace are very different. True, growth is growth wherever we find it, whether in the mineral, the vegetable, or the animal, but the principles and conditions on which growth depends are very different in the different spheres. Growth in all depends upon life; all life comes from God; therefore the power of growth, or the power to grow, must in all cases come from God. The lilies have no inherent power to thwart the Divine operation in developing their growth and lovely adornment. Man has this power, that is undoubted, and uses it to his own loss and destruction.

God is ever seeking to gain admittance into the man's heart, and when the door is opened, and God in the form of Divine Truth enters, the man does not then quietly fold his arms and wait till God makes him a new creature. God calls him to devote all the faculties and powers of his being to the new service. That while formerly he was in the service of the Devil, he must now be God's servant, by a faithful obedience to the commands of Christ. And the three great elements involved in this service are self-denial, carrying the cross, and following Christ; all of which require the continuous, active exercise of volition and fixed determination. And just in proportion as these are faithfully carried out, just in that proportion do we grow spiritually, and in no other way. Every sin resisted, every evil overcome, every act of self-denial for Christ's sake has its corresponding growth in grace. Every good and charitable act done for the good of others has its reward in the form of spiritual growth. This growth, like the kingdom of heaven, comes not by observation—it is within. The source of it also, like the wind which blows as it listeth, is not seen by observation; it, too, is within. You cannot tell whence it cometh, nor whither it goeth. But it is real, the kingdom of heaven is within. The parable of the lilies occurs both in Matthew and Luke, and in both cases essentially in the same connection, the difference in relationship being one of form only. In Matthew it is associated with the counsel to the disciples, " Lay not up to yourselves treasures upon earth, but lay up to yourselves treasures in heaven." And in Luke with the case of the rich man whose barns were full of goods, and who had made up his mind to eat, to drink, and to be merry—the conditions in both cases involving a life full of activity in the service of the Devil, the world, and the flesh. And the spiritual counsel in both cases involving the fullest exercise of all the faculties of our being to lay up the heavenly treasures, to be rich spiritually. This spiritual richness is spiritual growth. There can be no growth in grace whatever, without earnest persevering effort. Even to "be still" in the face of injury, provocation, or persecution, requires the exercise of the highest spiritual effort. The lilies toil not, they spin not; they require to do neither. They are perfect as God made them. They require no conversion, no regeneration, no struggle, no conflict. How different with man. " Seek ye first the kingdom," " Strive ye to enter," " Fight the good fight," " Press forward," " Labour not for the meat that perisheth, but labour to enter unto that rest," " Run the race." Thus, and thus only, will the Christian grow in grace, until he becomes clothed in robes more resplendent and beautiful than the adornments of the lily. Around the throne in heaven stand the faithful who have come through manifold temptations down here. And as we ask, " Who are these who stand clothed in bright array ? " we learn that these are they who have come through manifold tribulations and have washed their robes and made them white in the blood of the Lamb. Here and now, we are in the midst of these tribulations. Here and now we are washing our robes. What a labour, what an effort all this involves!

Not passively and automatically growing like mere plants, but fighting the good fight, bearing the cross, denying self.

In many parts of this Book, the idea that man is a mere automaton, or puppet, performing certain acts through strings in the hands of another is strongly indicated. In this chapter it is prominently seen. The professor says that in conversion there is a new principle introduced into the man; as he calls it a "living germ," and that this being "a germ of the Christ life must unfold into a Christ." This also may be a statement in harmony with scientific nomenclature: but it is decidedly misleading. If he really and truly means that a new principle, "a germ," is introduced into the person, and that that germ grows into a Christ, then the man himself has nothing to do in the matter. It is the germ that is to grow in grace and ultimately go to heaven; not the man. The man is nowhere, scarcely even an automaton. But the real question, and the only question to be answered, was—how was a man, a real man, to grow in grace? and the answer was, *he* was to grow as the lilies did. But now the subject is changed, and in place of the man growing, it is only a foreign germ introduced within him that grows.

Well, this might have been relevant enough, had it been shown that the lilies also grow by virtue of a germ introduced into their structure. Had this been done, it still might have been objected that in such a case, that the lilies did not grow, but only the introduced germ. Natural science when introduced into the spiritual sphere, often leads sadly astray. We know of no germs which grow in the man, but the germs of parasites. The man himself—the immortal soul under the guidance of God's truth—grows in grace, grows in goodness and wisdom, grows Godlike.

A number of valuable and interesting lessons are involved in this pictorial parable of the lilies which we cannot touch upon here. Christ did not explain *how* the lilies grow, for the simple reason that it was not a subject of lily culture. But the general lesson involved in it is simply this: do what is right under all circumstances, regardless of consequences, with a perfect assurance that all will ultimately be right. The disciples specially needed this counsel; so do we. They were called from their usual duties and avocations to a new work—a work which secured for them no monetary reward. And their prospect of subsistence must have been anything but bright or assuring. Food and raiment were absolutely essential for their bare existence, and how were these to be got? The illustration gives the answer, and contains the universal principle. The Divine call comes; let it be obeyed. No fears, no excuses. Follow me, is the command. Let nothing stand in the way. Let the dead bury their dead. Take no thought; the Lord will provide. "Seek ye first the kingdom of God and his righteousness," and all else necessary will be added. Consider the lilies. See that ye are in your right place, and be faithful. No anxiety, no worrying; growth, progress, and final reward are yours.

EPITOME.

The law which rules plant life in the natural sphere is entirely different from that which holds good in the spiritual sphere in growing in grace, for the three following reasons:

First. The plant always develops its own inherent ideal or character. In opposition to this, the Christian does not develop his own inherent character or ideal, but another and a very different character.

Second. The plant grows spontaneously. It takes no thought, makes no effort. In opposition to this, the Christian does take thought, earnest, serious thought, and is counselled and commanded to make effort. To work while it is day, to fight, to run, to lay up treasure.

Third. The flower and fruit of the natural plant appeals to the senses, and is here and now. In opposition to this, the flower and fruit of the Christian life is not sensuous, and is not here and now. The harvest is in heaven; the sheaves will all be seen there.

CHAPTER IV.

DEATH.

IN this chapter the professor labours under very considerable difficulties, no natural law of death having yet been discovered. But, in the absence of any natural law, he at once substitutes a mere verbal definition supplied by Herbert Spencer. The definition is a very hypothetical and a very abstruse one. In a condensed form, he says that life is " the continuous adjustment of internal relations to external relations," or, to be "in correspondence with its environments." Death, therefore, must be the reverse of this, namely, the want of adjustment of the internal to the external relations, or when an organism is not in correspondence with its environments.

After a number of illustrations of partial or complete want of correspondence, or partial or complete death in the natural plane, he proceeds to apply the same principle to the spiritual sphere. He shows, or assumes, that man is not in correspondence with the spiritual environment, and, taking that environment to mean God, that he is therefore not in correspondence with God. And this want of correspondence is spiritual death. In point of merit, we look upon this chapter as being weak compared to the others, and contains little that is in any way instructive. We shall therefore not dwell long over it.

Assuming that Spencer's definition of

death is correct, the issues from that doctrine are altogether irrelevant. Man stands in a certain relationship to the world without, by virtue of the peculiar structure of his organisation. He hears sound by virtue of an organ of hearing. He sees, tastes, and feels by virtue of organs fitted and adapted for these purposes. If by accident, or disease, his organ of hearing becomes impaired and the hearing is gone, we say the organ is dead, practically dead. But it would be perfectly absurd to say that the man was dead, and so of all his organs internal and external. When any organ ceases entirely to perform its functions we say *it* is dead, and this is exactly in keeping with what we have stated, namely, that we can predicate deadness only of something which exists, and which had been living, and not of something which had no existence, which would be an absurdity. Drummond wants to teach quite a different doctrine. He says in effect, that because a tree does not hear the singing of birds, nor sees the insects upon its branches, therefore, the tree is dead to these surroundings. This is an unwarranted use of the word. The tree never had any life in regard to seeing or hearing, and therefore, it never can be said to be dead in regard to these. And further, because the bird is unconscious of many things which man is conscious of and alive to, therefore it is dead to these. And further, that because a natural man is not in correspondence with the sphere above nature, namely, the spiritual sphere, he is therefore dead. Now really, though the language in which the professor clothes his ideas is most exact and scientific, there is in reality no analogy whatever, and no cohesion between the subjects. The tree never had any organ of seeing or hearing. The bird never had any organ for science or rationality, such as man has, and therefore in these respects they cannot be held to be dead in any sense. But man has a spiritual nature, and, at one time, that spiritual nature was in perfect correspondence with its spiritual environment, but, in the exercise of his freedom of will, he lost that correspondence, and as a consequence the whole of his spiritual faculties became disordered, and failed to discharge their intended functions. And it is this disordered and perverted state that is called spiritual death. The spiritual faculty however is there still, and may be restored to its proper use—made alive again. But no tree can ever be made to hear and see. There is no analogy between the two.

In the abstract, the professor seems to realise the terrible reality of spiritual death with its consequences, as taught in the Word; but, when the great reality is made to apply to unregenerated men of science, it is toned down to a very small thing indeed—a mere negation. Speaking of the word Death, he says it has "grown weak." "It carries with it no weight, no terror, it is ethically dead." No doubt, from a scientific point of view, it is dead. And so long as spiritual realities are looked at from a purely scientific point of view, so long will they be powerless. The tree is said to be dead as regards the environment of the bird, and the bird dead as regards the environment of the man, but neither the bird nor the tree can be blamed for that. It can be pronounced of them now, as at first—they are "very good." But the man, while out of harmony with God, is to blame for that, and it cannot be said of him now, that he is "very good." There is no analogy between the two.

The professor says: "We do not call the tree, nor the bird, a monster, because they are not in harmony with the environment above them," and for the same reason, he says, he would not call a man a monster, because he was out of harmony with the sphere above him—out of harmony with God, and while out of harmony, at direct antagonism with God, and all spiritual good. He tones down the solemn truth in a remarkable manner. The unregenerated scientific man is not a monster, but the professor says he may become "a dwarf." **Is** it possible that this is all the meaning that is involved as the outcome of spiritual death? That the man may become in the after life "a dwarf." The mole, doubtless, is quite happy without its eyes; and so are the fishes in the subterranean rivers—why may not the future dwarf? No wonder the word Death has lost its influence; who would fear to become a happy dwarf? But what does the Bible say: "The carnal mind is enmity against God," not a mere negation, but in direct antagonism against God. The unregenerated scientific man may not be a monster, but he certainly cannot be an angel. The Apostle John says: " In this the children of God are manifest, and the children of the Devil." A man becoming a child of the Devil is something like a monstrosity.

We regret exceedingly that the professor should have tried to square Christianity with Spencer's hypothetical reasonings. The whole of Spencer's system of sociology is a human invention. It ignores the necessity of revelation. It ignores the doctrine of the fall, of conversion and regeneration. It ignores man's dual nature, the natural and the spiritual, as well as all the solemn realities of the spiritual world. How can God's truth be made to harmonise with such a system, or any part of it?

EPITOME.

The law of Death, which holds good in the natural sphere, is entirely different from that which holds good in the spiritual sphere, in the three following particulars :

First. The natural organism which dies can never afterwards be made to live again. Opposed to this, we have the established truth, that a soul, though spiritually dead, can be made to live again.

Second. The natural organism after death becomes decomposed and resolved into its primary organic elements, and is forever annihilated as a natural organism. Opposed to this, we have the fact that the spiritual part of man, though perverted and depraved, is never decomposed in any sense, neither is it resolved into its primary elements.

Third. In natural death the organic functions cease entirely. Opposed to this, we have the sad fact that a soul, though spiritually dead, is still alive to sin, and in a state of active enmity against God. We therefore hold, that it is a fallacy to say that the same law applies to both; they are as opposite as day is to night.

CHAPTER V.

MORTIFICATION.

THE subject taken up in this chapter is closely affiliated to the one now finished, only, instead of Death absolutely, this has to do with killing or making to die. It forms a very interesting, and in many respects a very profitable, chapter to read. It contains, however, what we believe to be very serious errors, and starts from a very unsatisfactory basis. The scientific definition is from Herbert Spencer again, and the same as we had in the previous chapter—namely, that Death consists in "a falling out of correspondence with environment," which, in other words, simply means a man's organism not being suited to his surroundings; when this is the case, sooner or later the organism must go, must die; and this, as will be seen, constitutes the basis of the doctrine of mortification. In effect it teaches this: when the man becomes a Christian—becomes the recipient of eternal life—he finds that he must not any longer lead a selfish and a sinful life, but in place of that, one of self-denial and self-sacrifice, one of earnest and severe struggling and fighting against outward and internal temptations. But according to the professor, the man says, in place of being at all this pain and trouble, the best thing to do would be to die and go right off to heaven. The teaching in this connection is not perfectly clear, and being anxious not to misrepresent the author, we give his own words.

He says, "The moment the new life is begun there comes a genuine anxiety to break with the world." But the old refuses its dismissal. And as "it is clear that no man can attempt to live both lives," what is to be done in such an emergency? "A ready solution of this difficulty would be to die. But this alternative, fortunately or unfortunately, is not open. The detention here of body and spirit, for a given period, is determined for us, and we are morally bound to accept the situation." He says, "Bound to do it, willing or unwilling." But the ready solution would be to die and go to heaven. This appears to us to be ministering to a very prevalent, no doubt, but yet a very selfish, element in human nature. The universal desire is to get to heaven when we die. And the universal cry is,

"O that we could get some assurance that we would get to heaven after death." With such an assurance we would be quite happy. The desire to reach heaven is both the product of enlightened reason and the deepest instinct of our nature. It is also the will and purpose of God that we should, and therefore it is right. But the desire to go to heaven in order to avoid the discipline of life, with all its cares and struggles, is the product of moral cowardice. To all such, the assurance of getting to heaven rarely comes. Their hopes have no stable foundation to rest upon, hence they are always full of doubts and fears. There is no fear of any such, on reading this chapter, being tempted to commit real suicide in order to get at once to heaven. The fatal error here lies in looking perpetually for some outward heaven, and having no concern about the Christian's heaven, which must first be formed in the soul. It is a purely sensuous, not a spiritual, idea. It is like the delicate invalid, always suffering from external cold in his native country, thinking about some warm climate and anxious to get there to be warm—purely sensuous. This dying right off and going to heaven is a fallacy. No one can enter the gates of the holy city without being fitted and prepared for the holy companionship, and the holy life. Heaven must be begun here. Hence, in place of desiring to die right off, the desire ought to be all the other way. A desire to live to glorify God, to spend and be spent in his service, and to be of use to others, to testify and witness for Christ in the world. It is a deep delusion of our common enemy to imagine that, after serving the devil and the flesh during the best of our days, we may at last get into heaven without undergoing any spiritual change, without regeneration.

He then goes on to say that "Seeing we cannot die right off, the next best thing is to die piecemeal." This kind of dying we have presented to us under three heads—namely, suicide, mortification, and limitation. In each of these we think there is too much prominence given to the external act, and too little to the internal source of all sin. All the category of the sins of the flesh have their source in the depraved human heart— "Out of the heart proceed,"—and while it is of the greatest importance to avoid as far as possible all those external conditions which would in any way awaken latent depravity, still there is no security against outward transgression, no triumph over evil until the internal victory is achieved. Depravity is in the heart, and all regeneration must begin there. Make the fountain clean, and all the streams will be pure. He refers especially to the case of the drunkard, and gives this as a special instance where the cure lies external to the person—namely, as he puts it, by altering his environment. But we hold that unless there is first an internal break—namely, a break in the correspondence, all outward change will be a mere sham, and, like all other shams, soon come to an end. Recovery here, as in all other cases, must begin within and work outwards.

Under the head of Limitation, he takes up the evil of the love of money, and tones down that terrible curse in a very remarkable way. He says, "The love of money up to a certain point is a necessity; at what point, however, it must cease, each man has to determine for himself." Even so, and it is just because each man does determine this for himself, and to suit his own selfish ends, that the sin is so deep rooted and so wide spread. The love of money is a terrible evil. To what fearful depths of depravity has it not led! Every sin in the decalogue has been committed in order to satisfy the desire for money. Make money by fair means or foul, but make it. God says, the love of money is the root of all evil. We believe and accept that statement as one abundantly verified by fact. But a man's love of money is not to be measured by the amount of his possessions. In this race, love, though strong and ever ruling, is ofttimes blighted and its labour lost. A man may have much of this world's riches, and love them little; he may also have very little money, and love it very much. To work for money, not to love it, but to work for it, in order to purchase the necessaries of life, is a necessity binding upon all who are able. To work for money to support ourselves, and those dependent on us, is a binding Christian duty. And to work for money not only to support ourselves and those dependent upon us, but to assist in many ways those around us, is both a duty and a privilege.

The love of money, drunkenness, and bad temper to which he also refers, as well as all the other depravities, have their origin in the heart, and their basis in selfishness. The mere physical organization and its surroundings have very little to do in the matter. And yet in this chapter the professor puts it as if these were the all in all. He says, physical death "means the final stoppage of all correspondence with this sinful world." But as our life here is "determined for us," we must submit, and do the next best thing—namely, "if we cannot die altogether, the most we can do is to die as much as we can." We cannot admit this position. To say that mere physical death would put a stop to all our sinful correspondence is going too far. Living in the outer world does not in any sense constitute a sinful correspondence. The air we breathe, the ground we tread upon, and the sun which shines upon us are not sinful correspondences. Sin is a thing of the heart. A man's foes are those of his own household, and so long as these are there, mere physical death would not improve his correspondence.

A man becomes dead to sin and external evil, when he does not respond to its temptations. Not by committing suicide, not by mutilating his members, not by dying piecemeal. He dies by refusing to be led away by the sinful temptations of the flesh. The internal natural desires are not any more his masters. He brings all under the authority of Christ. He represses some, elevates others, regulates all, is the servant of none.

Then again, we do not admit that God determines the day of our death. God knows it, but He does not determine it. He does the very reverse. He gives us an organization fitted, adapted, and intended to do good and useful work; but man, as a rule, by his sin and folly shortens his days, and dies prematurely. He does it. The wicked do not live half their days, and the very best men certainly not their full complement. God does not determine the day of our death. We do it. Neither does God determine our spiritual death. We do it. Man-made creeds may teach another doctrine. We take God's everlasting testimony when He says, " Behold I set before you the way of life, and the way of death." Our choice, and ours alone, determines our fate.

CHAPTER VI.

ETERNAL LIFE.

The all important subject of eternal life treated of in this chapter is based upon another of Herbert Spencer's definitions. How the professor passes these definitions off as if they were laws, is a marvel. They have no claim whatever to be called "laws." The definition is this: " Perfect correspondence would be perfect life. Were there no changes in the environment but such as the organism had adapted changes to meet, and were it never to fail in the efficiency with which it met them, there would be eternal existence and eternal knowledge." And from this he endeavours to substantiate the doctrine that the man, having received the gift of eternal life, is thereby in harmony with the spiritual environment, and must live for ever. Of course he contends that this living for ever includes something more, namely, the quality of the source of the eternal life. He speaks of Spencer's definition as a "startling achievement," something for which the world should be profoundly thankful; as if it had been something substantial that had been discovered, something that was to benefit the race. In place of that, it never can be of the slightest value to any human being whatever. The definition helps to nothing—gives nothing. Referring to Christ's doctrine of eternal life, he says: "Apart from revelation, this great truth was unguaranteed." But now he says:

"Here at last comes, and comes unbidden, an opportunity of testing the most vital point of the Christian system." This is an extraordinary position in which to put Christ's doctrine of eternal life. As if, forsooth, the guarantee of its truthfulness rested upon its harmonising with Herbert Spencer's definition! This is rather humiliating, to say the least of it. We see nothing in Spencer's definition to call forth either admiration or gratitude. It is a mere verbal definition—nothing more. A hungry soul wants *food*, not a definition of digestion or assimilation.

We cannot admit Spencer's definition of eternal life in any sense as a test of the "vital point" in our religion. The actual experience only of those who have come under its power is of any value as a test—not that of Herbert Spencer, who denies the whole fabric of Christianity. In every nation, in every rank and station in life, individual Christians have had the test and witness of the vital point in Christianity in their own experience. As a test of a speculative system of theology, Spencer's definition may be applied; but it bears no relationship whatever to practical Christianity.

At page 215, he says, "To know God is to correspond with God." This is one of the professor's bold statements, which, by its very boldness, evades criticism. We cannot grant this. To know God is not necessarily to correspond with God. Far from it. To know God implies something in our constitution in some way affiliated to God. This affiliation lies in the still existing remains of the Divine image and likeness in every one.

But for this there could be no knowledge of God whatever. The mere higher animal could never be made to know God. And as this constitutes the power by which we can know God, it is evident that it must be there before the knowledge, and that therefore it is not a product of that knowledge. The first effect of this knowledge is not only *not* to correspond with God, but to enable us to see and realise to what a terrible extent we do not correspond. And it is a matter of fact now, and in all past ages of the Church of Christ, that thousands of the best and truest Christians that ever lived have had this realisation more or less to the end of their life on earth. This is a truth of experience. The professor's statement is a mere scientific inference.

Another of these sweeping statements is found at page 215, where, after referring to the artist and the musician, he says, "To find a new environment again and cultivate it, is to find a new life." This really is reducing a solemn subject to a mere flower of speech. Such a person finds no new life, but a new channel or field for the life he already had. In several parts of this chapter we think the non-immortality of the wicked is clearly indicated, though he is careful not to commit himself to the doctrine. He says the gift of eternal life "includes everlastingness." If this is so, then the absence of it must necessarily exclude it. There would be no need for including everlastingness *in* the gift, if the recipient had it naturally. Speaking of the spirit of Sonship, he says, "This is not an

Reply to Drummond. 91

organic, but a spiritual correspondence." This is a very feeble and unmeaning distinction. If the spiritual correspondence is genuine, it must be organic. It cannot be merely ideal or one of implication. It must be actual. And as he says at page 239 that, "the soul is a living organism," surely the transformation which makes a dead organism a living organism must be organic

After showing that the new spiritual environment is eternal life, he says, "This is a correspondence which at once satisfies the demands of science and religion." If this is so, if the demands of science are so thoroughly satisfied, and the whole spiritual system so scientifically demonstrated, how does he account for the fact that scientific men still reject it *in toto* and call it a biological conceit.

EPITOME.

The natural view of eternal life, as laid down by Herbert Spencer and adopted by Professor Drummond, is entirely different from the view of eternal life as taught in God's Word. You remember Spencer's definition—namely, that unfailing ability to alter one's condition, or the correspondence to meet every possible change in the environment.

First. In Heaven character is fixed, and can undergo no change in quality, therefore the correspondence can undergo no spiritual change. It can only progress.

Second. As God is unchangeable, the environment as represented by Him can undergo no change. He can only unfold or reveal Himself more fully.

Third. As the relationship between the correspondence and the environment is one of fixed harmony, there can be no necessity for any unfailing power to meet the changes in the environment by a similar change in the correspondence.

CHAPTER VII.

ENVIRONMENT.

The chief object aimed at in this chapter is to prove that a man's character is decided by his organisation and his surroundings. This is the favourite standpoint of the materialist. Drummond says, "heredity and environment are the master influences of the organic world. Heredity and environment have made us what we are. In the spiritual world also, the subtle influences which form and transform the soul are heredity and environment." So that a man spiritually is just the creature of his organisation, which he derives from his parents, modified by surroundings. This is his creed; and there can be no doubt that he is in this respect perfectly at one with all the materialistic men of the age. They all hold this doctrine. The professor's cure for all the spiritual evils in life is to change our environment. This is all we can do. For, he holds that the heredity evil we have no control over. In detail, he says, "The cardinal error in the religious life is to attempt to live without an environment. What is the spiritual environment? It is God." And further, that we receive from this environment all we need for living a true and perfect life, and that our receptivity depends upon a simple union between the organism and the environment.

The fundamental principle running through the whole chapter is, that our only business is to change the environment. That is to say, that the change which is to transform a non-Christian into a Christian—an unbeliever into a believer—a bad man into a good man—is an outside change. From this we must dissent. On the natural plane it is true that this is all that can be done in improving the breed and condition of animals. And great changes have been effected in this way. You must alter their surroundings. Spiritually it is just the reverse. It is the person that must be changed—or, in the language of science, the correspondence. It is in the correspondence alone that *the* change must take place if ever a sinner is to become a saint, or a non-Christian, a Christian. The environment may, as a rule, be safely left alone. The natural man is blind to spiritual things, and his eyes must be opened. He is deaf to spiritual things, and his ears must be unstopped. The spirit of conversion is that the man is changed. There is no use in objecting to this by saying that God must *first* come, and that He must *first* act. He is *always* doing so. There is no use in trying to put the blame on the environment. The universal environment is God, and from this there is no escaping—neither here nor hereafter. The fool hath said in his heart, and many others have tried to say in their reason, no God. But consciously or unconsciously he environs everyone. The blame and the whole blame is man's.

It may be contested that all this is involved in man's power to change his environment; but our answer to that is that in changing his environment, *he* must turn to the spiritual environment. He must look to the source and fountain of life and light, formerly he was looking away from, formerly he was turned the other way. This turning *to* is a change of correspondence spiritually. "Turn ye, turn ye, why will ye die?" It is spiritually the very same principle as was involved in the case of the drunkard. He never can alter the environment— break off the habit—until he personally internally has undergone a change, which really is a change of correspondence.

Drummond allows that man has the power to change his environment, but this is all the power he does allow. But it is absurd to say that a man can possibly choose the service of God, until his mind is first made up to break with the world. *The* reason and the only reason why a converted man wishes to change his environment is, because his correspondence is entirely changed ; and that therefore the old environment will not now suit. But not only so, after the correspondence has been changed, and the environment changed to suit that ; the new born Christian will find that the new environment, though consciously new to him now, had ever been about him, ever present with him and active. Not like the singing of the bird to the tree, for the singing of the bird had no influence whatever on the tree : but active, operating and controlling. He will see and realize numberless instances in which God had led, sustained, and delivered him. He did not then know it, but it was real and true for all that. Not like the poor consumptive going to a far distant land for a more genial climate—no, nothing like that. God had always been with him. That environment had always been about him.

In the course of this chapter, he refers to the clay and the potter, and says that there are as many potters as there are forms of life. Correctly speaking, this is not so. There is only one Potter—only one Creator. And of all vessels which God has made and into which he has breathed life only one—namely man—has had the power to blurr and vitiate his workmanship, and even to turn round and ask the Potter, why hast thou made me thus?—man has a power which no other creature has.

He also takes up the subject of heredity influence. But this opens up too large a subject to treat of here. We would just say this much, that heredity does not supersede or destroy our responsibility. A man is not the creature of his physical organisation. The organisation has its influence on the manifestation of character—that is undoubted. But the man himself is above his organisation. The philosophy underlying this important subject is to be found in this direction. We derive the natural part of our being from our parents, and that has capabilities or tendencies to evil. But we get the soul from God, not from our parents. And the soul or spiritual part of our being has the determining choice of following after the tendencies of the lower nature, "the law in the members," or, of resisting it. And the soul, being the *real man*, is responsible for the choice he makes. Let us ever hold by this—that

God made the *you* and the *me*, as really and truly as he made Adam. Our parents do not make us. But they have all to do with our bodies, and that is a great deal. The proclivities we inherit, exist as organic capabilities; but their outgrowth does not take place with the certainty of a natural law. Nothing like that. When it does take place, the fact is specially noticed. The tendency to drunkenness has been adduced in this connection; but we often, very often, find that parents who have been given to excess, have been succeeded by children who are total abstainers. True, it has been said that this is brought about by a moral revulsion on the part of the children. But we do not find that physical heredity taints, such as scrofula, cancer, or consumption, are ever arrested or cured by corresponding physical revulsions in the experience of those who have been so unfortunate as to inherit such taints. Natural laws are very unbending, very exacting. It would be dreadful to think that anything approaching to this could hold good in the spiritual sphere. Thank God it is not so.

Man is not only not the creature of his organisation, but he is something far above it. Though the body is beautifully and wonderfully suited to man's wants and uses in this world, its organic capacities by no means adequately represent, nor do they fully satisfy, the capacities of the soul. In every direction man feels that his spiritual aspirations far transcend the actual capacities of his organisation. And this of itself proves that these aspirations and desires cannot be the product of that organisation. Look at the organ of vision alone as an example. Wonderful, extensive and varied as that organ is, yet how very imperfectly does it of itself fulfil our desires and longings. And to what a vast extent have we been able by scientific skill and ingenuity to supplement that organ by optical instruments— the telescope and the microscope. And marvellous as are these aids, we are not yet satisfied, we want something more powerful still.

Look also at our organic powers of locomotion. How simple, how varied, and how nimble these often are; and yet how very inadequately do they meet and satisfy our wants. The felt need, the felt craving for something far greater, far more powerful than our mere organic powers are capable of, has led us to supplement these limitations, by means of steam ships and locomotive engines, besides many other forms of machinery, to do work for which our natural organic powers are altogether unfitted. And yet, we want more power, and greater speed. Look also at the telephone, to supplement our organ of hearing, and the printing press to supplement our powers of writing.

The same is true of our spiritual visions and aspirations. Our natural organic faculties do not, by any means, fully meet and satisfy these. Man is limited, restricted by his organisation, "cribbed, cabined, and confined." And it is only when that organisation is put off, that he can ever find a full scope for, and a perfect realisation of, all his spiritual desires. The instinctive wants and capa bilities of the animal creation are the product of their organisation, and consequently their wants and capacities are perfectly fulfilled by that organisation. They have no upward, onward, progressive aspirations such as man has. One race makes no advance or improvement on the attainments of its predecessors. How very different to this is the history of the human race, and who can doubt that it was intended by our Creator, that all these spiritual aspirations and capacities were not only to be duly cultivated, but ultimately to be fully satisfied. And still further, we must conclude that just in so far as we follow the Divine order, the Divine plan, to that extent will these aspirations be realised, and give some foretaste and fore-shadowing of what will be in the coming future, when this mortal organisation shall have been put off, and we are clothed with our spiritual body. Scientists may say that man is the creature of his physical organisation. We hold he is far above it.

This chapter is closed with the following statement: "Where do organisation and environment meet? How does that which is becoming perfect avail itself of its perfecting environment, and the answer is just as in nature. The condition is simple receptivity: and yet this is perhaps the most simple of all conditions. It is so simple that we will not act upon it." There are a great many euphonistic utterances throughout the book. This is one of them. When he says that, " We will not act upon it." One feels in a doubt as to whether anybody acts upon it at all; or if it is only a certain class of people who will not act upon it. What he really means by receptivity in the spiritual sphere, he does not condescend to explain. But, if it has just the same significance as receptivity in the natural sphere, then it can have no moral quality whatever. He adds: "Christ has condensed the whole truth into one memorable sentence, namely this, 'As the branch cannot bear fruit of itself except it abide in the vine; no more can ye except ye abide in Me. He that abideth in me, the same bringeth forth much fruit.'" In this beautiful quotation there is apparently the element of receptivity coupled with passivity, but it is only apparent. The entire passage involves the highest exercise of the will and affection of the spiritual man; and this is more forcibly brought out in a verse further down the chapter, which the professor conveniently does not quote, namely an explanation *how* they were to abide in the vine; and this abiding in the vine was the vital point. How was this to be secured? "If ye keep My commandments, ye will abide in Me." Here lies the secret of the difficulty; and the reason why we will not act upon it—Simple receptivity? *No, no;* earnest, continuous effort, self-denial, cross-bearing.

EPITOME.

The law of heredity and environment, which holds good in the natural sphere, does not hold good in the spiritual sphere, in the three following particulars:

First. In the case of Adam, there was a perfect heredity and a perfect environment, and yet, by the exercise of his freedom of will, he fell—stained his character.

Second. Every man is conscious, in view of his surroundings—his environment—and also in view of his own capacities, his heredity—of having done wrong. Every man, the most depraved and most perverted, does blame himself for having done what he knows he should not have done. That is to say that he had the power, and ought to have done otherwise.

Third. That under the worst heredity, and under the worst environment, men have turned to God and become new creatures. Heredity and environment do not make the man.

CHAPTER VIII.

CONFORMITY TO TYPE.

The great object the professor has in view in this chapter, is to show that like produces its like by virtue of a natural law which has received this title—Conformity to Type. According to this law, " everything which comes into this world is compelled to stamp upon its offspring the image of itself." And this law, he says, holds good in the spiritual sphere, and is proved in the fact that the living Christ enters the human soul and works there, producing His own image, and thereby conformity to Christ's type. Throughout the whole of this chapter we have strongly marked one of the most saddening elements of the Calvinistic theology, namely, that man has nothing to do in the working out of his Christian life and character; that Christ in the man does it all for him. We need not go over in detail all the arguments in this chapter. They have been already discussed. It contains nothing new.

God made man for His own glory, and that he as a creature should in his finite capacity be a partaker of the Divine character, and, as a consequence, be happy. The nature and constitution of his being fitted him for this purpose. All his powers were God-given, given to be used as his own, yet not self-originated, given and constantly sustained by his God. By the exercise of his freedom of will he misused his God-given faculties and marred the Divine purpose, the result being moral depravity, physical disease and suffering, estrangement from God. Still God never changed His purpose, but continued to manifest His Fatherly love and care for His children, manifesting Himself in ways and forms adapted to man's special wants to restore him to his right allegiance. Every means which love and wisdom could devise, consistent with man's moral nature, have been used for this purpose at sundry times and in divers manners, culminating in the fullest and last manifestation or revelation of His will and purpose in the Divine Incarnation.

In all these manifestations, God has ever recognised man's ability to know, to love, and to obey his God. For, though man had abused and perverted his God-given faculties, yet God had never taken these from him; and now as a Father, a Friend, and a Brother, He is striving with the race to redeem and to save it. He stands at the door of every heart knocking for admittance. He entreats, He pleads with His creatures to turn from the evil of their ways, to come and receive a Father's forgiveness and a Father's blessing, and again enter into His love and service. Every means are used, every help given, and it is at the individual's own peril that he turns a deaf ear. And to those who do obey His call, He gives special help and strength to fight against and overcome all their spiritual enemies, and to live to His glory. And, thank God, many have in all ages obeyed the call and returned to a Father's home. And while, on the great day of accounts, all will joyfully acknowledge that there was no merit whatever in anything they had done—no merit in doing what it was their highest duty and privilege to do—God Himself will pronounce upon them the most precious of all rewards: "Well done, good and faithful servant, enter thou into the joy of thy Lord."

In teaching the doctrine of man's inability to turn to God and serve Him, the professor refers to the case of the potter and the clay, and shows that as the clay does not make the vessel, but that God does, therefore God makes the Christian in the same way as the potter makes the vessel. Now, just mark the captious and misleading way in which this argument is put. There is no dispute about God being *the* Potter, nor as to the fact of His making all vessels; but a Christian and a vessel are by no means convertible terms, and yet the professor uses them as such. A Christian man is a vessel having a special quality of character, and we hold that he makes, and that he alone is responsible for the making of, that character. With the vessel he has nothing to do—with the character he has everything to do. God made all the vessels in heaven and in hell; but He did not make their characters in the same way as the potter makes the clay into vessels. A man becomes a child of the Evil one by disobeying God and voluntarily choosing the service of the Devil. He becomes a Christian, a child of God, by obeying God and voluntarily choosing and faithfully following his master Christ, and in no other way.

One of the worst features of all religious controversies is that of adducing one part of Scripture to defeat or overturn another, and not for the purpose of elucidation. We have a marked example of this in connection with this subject in his quotation of that well known verse, " Work out your own salvation with fear and trembling, for it is God that worketh in you." The professor affirms that the latter clause of the verse was added in order to prevent any " misconception," to prevent any one from thinking that he had any power to work out his own salvation, for he has none. God alone has the power. Now, in place of the second clause being added to prevent any misconception, surely every unprejudiced reader will see that it was given for an entirely different purpose: namely, as the strongest inducement, the highest encouragement, to work; that in this great work he was not alone, but that he had God on his side, the Spirit of God within him, and, with that, to have perfect assurance that his work would be crowned with success.

Again, the professor tries to establish the doctrine that man is a mere automaton by referring to various functions of his natural body over which he has no control, and holds that the same is true in the spiritual sphere. His illustrations are very misleading and not true. He says man has "no control over the action of the heart, his breathing, his digestion," &c. We hold that he has most distinctly, and just in the same way that he has had control over his spiritual functions. These functions he cannot create—that is undoubted; but he can pervert and vitiate every one of them. Every organ and every function in his body man has brought into a diseased condition. From the crown of his head to the sole of his foot he is diseased. Every individual man has not every disease, but the race has been and is so diseased. We cannot make the power which animates those organs; but by breaking the laws of our being, we pervert the functions and alter the organs. An automaton has no such power as this —none. And God holds every man responsible for the use he makes of this power. Man is not a mere automaton in any sense, but a free and responsible agent. God made him such, and God deals with him as such always. Every one is endowed with certain faculties, and these he can use or not, just as he chooses.

This is a practical fact everyone knows to be true.

Every man has certain desires or wishes, and he wills to act, and in the great majority of cases does act, in view of these desires. It is true that circumstances may be against him—dead against him—and he sees that it would be hopeless to attempt anything. But it is just in these very cases where his liberty and freedom of choice is seen most conspicuously, and he feels that, but for the special hindrance, his conduct would certainly be in such a particular way. The experience of every man, woman, and child, proves that we are all free agents. Every one has been in doubt and difficulty as to what should be done. Most of us have passed through, not only difficulty, but severe conflict, in view of duty. No mere automaton, no mere passive agent, could ever experience anything of this kind.

It is in this personal freedom or conscious selfhood of the man that we have the seat and the source of all sin. Without this there could be no consciousness of sin—none. And it is just in proportion as a person realises this perfect freedom, this personal, individual ownership of all his faculties, that he ever can have any realisation of personal sinfulness, and consequently be in the very first stage a recipient of Divine grace. Conviction of sin is the first effect of the Divine operation; but without the inherent freedom and the conscious power to have acted otherwise, conviction of sin would be an impossibility. And the great struggle in life with every Christian is to subdue and gain the victory over this terrible power of freedom to feel and do for self. And the final victory of every Christian is when, by the grace of God, under the influence of Divine truth, he succeeds in substituting God's will in place of his own will. But a perfect surrender of self to the will of God is only possible when self has been fully realised as a living rebel against God, and this self-surrender in every case implies the highest exercise of the will. This will is never taken away; but, in a perfectly regenerated state, in a heavenly state, it must ever yield a loyal obedience to the will of God.

EPITOME.

The natural law of conformity to type, by which every living thing is " compelled to stamp upon its offspring the image of itself," does not hold good in the spiritual sphere for the following three reasons :

First. Both the protoplasm* and the vital force which determine the future animal are the immediate and the direct product of the parents of that animal. In direct opposition to this, the protoplasm in the man—as described by Drummond, into which Christ enters, and on which He operates, is a product of the man himself, and not of God.

Second. The protoplasm of the animal has not only no power to desire and cry for the animal life, but it has no power

---

* The introduction of the word protoplasm, which is purely speculative in its character, into the realm of spiritual things, we cannot but look upon as a dangerous innovation, and one not at all calculated to throw any light on any spiritual truth, but only to mystify and darken it.

to resist. The very reverse of this is true spiritually. The man has the power to cry for, and also the power to resist.

Third. While the animal is "compelled" to stamp its image on its offspring, the very reverse is true in the spiritual sphere. God comes to us in love, pure love. He operates in and on us, not by compulsion, but as an act of pure *free grace.* There are other obvious reasons, but these, we consider, are sufficient to destroy all analogy or identity.

CHAPTER IX.

SEMIPARASITISM AND PARASITISM.

The two chapters under these respective headings, are in some respects the best in the whole book, and cannot fail to be read with the greatest interest.

Parasites in the vegetable and animal world have this element in common, get a place of safety, a place to live in, and sustenance, without doing anything for either, safety and support at the expense of others. This principle also holds good in the spiritual sphere. And although the professor condemns the doctrine in very strong terms as a doctrine, he very innocently ignores the fact that he himself had laid the foundation for the doctrine, and taught it in the chapter on conformity to type, and, indeed, all through the book this doctrine is specially taught. The general tenor is this—Man can do nothing in the matter of his soul's salvation—God does not require him to do anything. Christ makes the Christian, as the potter makes vessels out of the dead, passive clay. Only get hold of Christ, and he will do all for us. We are to " permit " Christ to do all for us —passively to " submit " to be made like Christ. True, he admits that man has something to do in the initial stage, but no more. Now this is just the character of the parasite all through. The parasite does something at first—the initial act is by it. It gets hold of the shell of the whelk, which was not its own, and like a mean poltroon is content with that. And in this shell it neither works for food nor anything. The mistletoe also takes the initiative by seizing hold of the tree, and there it lives on the fruit of another's labour for its support. It does nothing.

The professor says that our Churches are "overflowing with parasites." That may be true in his experience; we cannot endorse it. The mere fact that a congregation imbibes the truths which have been eliminated by the toil and study of the minister, and to which they have contributed nothing, does not by any means constitute the members of that congregation parasites. In every department of science, of literature and art, if ever we are to learn anything at all, we must be dependent on the labours of others. No one is born with any kind of knowledge, and whatever branch of study we turn to, we must, in the first place, be entirely dependent upon the labours of others. This is also true of man as a human being. The infant can do nothing but imbibe that for which it has not laboured, and it must for years be entirely dependent upon the labour of others for the supply of its needs. But we never think of calling children parasites for all that.

It is in the very nature of the parasite to be what it is. We take it that the professor's definition of a parasite is defective. The essential element in the character of the parasite is that while it imbibes nourishment for which it has not laboured, it consumes that upon its own being, and gives out nothing in return. This giving out nothing in return is the essence of the parasite. That there are moral and spiritual parasites, we have no doubt whatever; but that our churches are overflowing with such we do not believe. Few if any members of our churches act fully up to their duty. God only knows the true state of every man. A truly Christian life consists in a giving out, and embodying in the daily walk and conversation, that life of purity, uprightness and charity which makes a man Christ-like. It is not a matter of intellectual notions about religion—nor of literary or scientific attainments.

The whole of this subject is a severe satire on our ministers, our church members, and our theology. He distinctly says that "many churches exist for the very purpose of making and collecting spiritual parasites." We do not believe this to be true. And while he admits that a very few members get benefit in churches, he says churches overflow with members whose only interest in religion is parasitic. Where spiritual parasites go to in the after life he does not say. The satire is much too severe, and altogether unwarranted. Were it at all justifiable, the right thing to do would be to burn all our theological books, disband our ministers, and close our church doors.

The professor is very severe in his condemnation of all kinds of theological formulæ, because these profess to give a systematic and concise view of theology. What he says would be equally applicable to the most concise and condensed formula we have, as given in the Lord's Prayer, or in the Sermon on the Mount. He says, theological formulæ lead to "spiritual paralysis," but the form in which truth is presented in the Bible prevents any possibility of this. "Truth in the Bible is a fountain." We question the correctness of the similitude. No three individuals could go to the same fountain, and draw three different kinds of water; but thirty different individuals will go to the Bible and bring away thirty different kinds of creeds. It is not like a fountain, but it is very like an immense quarry, many of the stones in which are precious and valuable, and the rule is that every man who wants a spiritual house goes to that quarry and digs, chisels, and hews stones suitable to the kind of house he wants to build. And of these stones, out of that one quarry, what a variety of houses are built! What grotesque and strange structures are erected!

EPITOME.

The law of parasites in the natural sphere is entirely different from the law of parasites in the spiritual sphere in the three following particulars:

First. In the natural sphere, once a parasite, ever a parasite. In opposition to this, a spiritual parasite may change.

Second. In the natural sphere a parasite is such from necessity. In the spiritual sphere a man is so from deliberate choice —very much so.

Third. In the natural sphere a parasite is so, for a present and an immediate good. In opposition to this, the spiritual parasite is so, in prospect of a future good.

CHAPTER X.

CLASSIFICATION.

This is by far the most laboured and unsatisfactory part of the book, while at the same time it deals with subjects of the very highest importance. At the outset the professor wishes to show the radical distinction between a Christian and a non-Christian, and applies as his test the same law which he laid down in the natural sphere—namely, that the mineral was separated from the vegetable by a sharp and impassable line of demarcation; and these two were also separated from the animal by a line equally well marked, by reason of which the one could never become the other. The same law holds good, he says, in the spiritual sphere.

The three great divisions under which the whole creation is arranged is decided by what the professor calls classification, and each division has its separate sphere and function in life. The properties which it possesses, and the phenomena which it is capable of manifesting, are determined by the class to which it belongs. In other words, the classification determines its character. We dissent from this altogether.

To start with, he takes two specimens of earth; the one from the Island of Arran, and the other from the Island of Barbadoes. The one consists of fine crystals of silica; the other of fine shells or urns, the product of a small animal.

Both of these, the crystals and the shells, are very beautiful when carefully examined under the microscope; so much so, that it is difficult to say which of the two is most to be admired. But, he says, there is this essential difference between the two, the shell is the product of life, the other is dead; and for this reason they represent two different classes—the living and the dead; and the beauty of the one is therefore separated from the beauty of the other by a line of demarcation as distinct as that which separates the living from the dead. The reasoning on this point is exceedingly weak. The shells were the product of life; but where, we ask, did the crystals come from? What made them? Did they make themselves, or did death make them? We say they were the product of life. God made the crystals. The animals only moulded the shells out of material made by God.

He speaks about the law of crystallisation in contradistinction to the law of life. But what is the law of crystallisation but just the mode and manner of the Divine operation in these particles of matter? The silica has no determining power of its own to assume any particular form. None. Its power is fixed and determined by God. He speaks about chemistry making crystals and of reproducing crystals. That is not so. The simple fact is, you cannot prevent the crystals forming; and that property or power by which the silica always takes on its special crystalline form is its life.

In connection with classification, he draws a clear distinction between the Christian and the not-a-Christian, on the ground of the spiritual difference between what he calls, "Moral and Spiritual Beauty." Now really, moral and spiritual beauty are very vague and flexible terms. Beauty is not a property or quality of anything, but rather a sentiment called up in the mind of an observer by certain qualities or attributes in something observed. To have made the subject tangible and definite, he should have stated the qualities or attributes which were beautiful; but this he has not done. And yet he looks upon the distinction between moral and spiritual beauty as being a vital one. He says, "Moral beauty is the product of the natural man—spiritual beauty the product of the spiritual man; and these two, according to the law of Biogenises, are separated from one another by the deepest line known to science." His distinction between moral and spiritual beauty is a fallacy, and clearly necessitated by the demands of materialistic science. All through, the professor denies the spiritual part of humanity; but this we must defend. And from this point of view we would say that moral beauty is the operation and manifestation of the inner man in the outer life. And spiritual beauty is the operation which takes place *within* the man, known and recognised as the motives and principles from which the outer act proceeds. The real quality of the man, and the quality of the act, depend entirely upon the nature of the interior motives.

It is sad to think that the professor so persistently ignores man's spiritual nature. The whole of God's Word is addressed not only to man as a spiritual being, but it is addressed to, and can be apprehended and understood only by, the spiritual part of his being. A material organisation can realise and apprehend only material things. All the functions of our material organisation are bounded by the wants of the organisation; and these wants are only material—God, Heaven, Eternity and the Judgment, have no meaning to a being that is only material. A material organisation has no hope, no thought of anything beyond the grave. The Bible everywhere appeals to the heart and conscience. It has special regard to the inner motives of our life, and recognises in these motives the true quality of all character—these motives are the activities of the spiritual being, not of the brain.

Following out his theory of natural law in the spiritual world, the professor in this chapter comes to the conclusion that the Heavenly Kingdom is to be the *smallest* of all other kingdoms. At page 410 he says: "The broad impression gathered from the utterance of the Founder of the spiritual kingdom is that the number of organisms to be included in it is to be comparatively small— "*Quantity decreases as quality increases.*" Can this really be so? Is the spiritual kingdom, the kingdom of the saved, the redeemed, the blest and the happy, to be the smallest of all the other kingdoms? Is such an idea consistent with the known character and attributes of God—a God of infinite love, and of infinite resources? We cannot believe it. No, rather perish every form of natural science and philosophy than lead us to such a conclusion as this.

The yearnings and the strivings of the good and the true in all ages, have been to bring about the greatest amount of good to the greatest number; and men have failed hitherto, and do still fail, because they have not the power to give effect to their desires, and because they have not the knowledge of the right ways and means by which to accomplish these desires. Ignorance, selfishness, and depravity still predominate; pain, suffering and sorrow are still the prevailing lot of the race. But God's Word gives us sure grounds for believing that there is still a good time in store for the race. "Thy kingdom come," is not simply a prayer taught, it is the expression of a want engraven in the depths of our being, and, until that kingdom does come, that want must still be there, and be felt, though men may not understand its true meaning.

Political reformers with high sounding phrases, and large promises, have been and are still, trying to fill up the want by trying to introduce their form of kingdom. Men of science are trying their systems of natural evolution and gradual development. Philosophical sociology, with its ignoring of God and denial of revelation, is also, after its fashion, aiming at the same end. But all these must fail. Society will never, by any nor all of these means, become better, but worse. And whenever the Christian system becomes affiliated to and identified with these human systems, we may look for a more wide-spread development of selfishness, sensuality, and spiritual blindness. But even then, and just then, new light will come, a higher, a fuller, and more perfect revelation from God will come, which will lead on to a full realisation and fulfilment of the prayer, "Thy kingdom come." Already foreshadowings and foregleams of that golden age are piercing and cleaving through the thick darkness and entering human hearts. The dawn of that glorious morn is drawing near, though the full and perfect day must be far in the future. Still we shall pray, "Thy kingdom come."

Moral, spiritual, and intellectual darkness have long reigned, and do still reign, over a large portion of our globe, but we have the assurance in God's word that the earth " shall be filled with the knowledge of the glory of the Lord, as the waters cover the sea." Yes, on this present earth; and there shall be no exception, for, "All the ends of the world shall remember and turn unto the Lord; and all the kindreds of the nations shall worship before Thee," and, "All the ends of the earth shall see the salvation of our God." Horrid cruelty, wicked wars and cruel oppression, have long prevailed in the world, and they still prevail; but the time must come when men, "Shall beat their swords into ploughshares, and their spears into pruning hooks. Nation shall not lift up a sword against nation, neither shall they learn war any more." And this will not be brought about by any human expedient or device which may be made one day and broken the next—it will be of Divine origin, stable and permanent in its duration. "He shall have dominion also from sea to sea, and from the river unto the ends of the earth. His name shall endure for ever. His name shall be continued as long as the sun." And that shall be a happy, a peaceful, and a prosperous time, for all men will be holy. "The meek shall inherit the earth." "I will make thy officers peace, and thine executors righteousness. Violence shall no more be heard in thy land, wasting nor destruction within thy borders; but thou shalt call thy walls salvation, and thy gates praise." "In that day shall there be upon the bells of the horses, 'Holiness unto the Lord.'" "In his days shall the righteous flourish, and abundance of peace so long as the moon endureth."

Then shall be realised the song of the angels "on earth peace, good-will among men." For this God veiled His glory and took upon himself our nature and lived as a man among men. For this he bore the sins of the world, submitted to the buffeting, the reproaches, and the scourgings of wicked men; and at last died an ignominious death on the cross. For this, bards have sung, prophets taught, saints and martyrs suffered and bled. For this ten thousand prayers ascend every day to the throne in the heavens; and for this the whole creation groans and travails, "Thy kingdom come." And as this shall be an everlasting kingdom—because the only kingdom which can adequately and intelligently embody and reflect the image and likeness of its King and Founder— the numbers which shall be gathered in from it to the upper Spiritual Kingdom in the heavens, will, as the countless ages roll on, be such as vastly to transcend in greatness all other kingdoms which have ever existed. With this faith and this hope we shall ever pray, " Thy kingdom come."

At the close of this chapter, referring to that "supreme law" which has been moulding the universe and all it contains at will, he describes it as directing the evolutions of those million peopled worlds as if they were simple " cells or organisms," and further that man's "organism" must pass through all the stages of differentiation and integration, growing in perfectness and beauty under the wider, the unfolding of the higher evolution until it reaches the " Infinite complexity—the Infinite sensibility." This is the goal to which Drummond's Natural Law in the Spiritual world is to lead us. What that goal means in reality we must leave others to judge. We can know something of the Divine man, the man, Christ Jesus—the Elder Brother; but of the Infinite complexity and the Infinite sensibility we know nothing. We can love our Father in Heaven, but to love the Infinite complexity or the Infinite sensibility is to talk nonsense.

EPITOME.

The Law of Classification, as determining character in the Natural sphere, does not hold good in the spiritual sphere in the three following essential elements :

First. The Classification of man does not determine his character, not in the least—God made man in his own image and likeness, and thereby classified him for Heaven. All the elements in his being—all the capabilities of his organisation, were such as would make him capable of being fitted and prepared for a heavenly home. But that classification did not determine his character.

Second. Reason and revelation alike warrant us in saying that in opposition to the Divine classification, man made his own character—what that character has been we all know. In the natural sphere no animal determines its own character.

Third. Man has still the power to re-determine his character, and it is the whole purpose and scope of revelation that he should do so. And God holds him guilty if he does not. There is nothing like this in the natural sphere.

We have now got to the end of Professor Drummond's Natural Law in the Spiritual World, and would in conclusion only add one or two sentences.

The radical error occurs in the first

chapter. When the plant seizes hold of the mineral, and the animal seizes hold of the plant, that is not done with the object of making the mineral to live, nor yet to give the plant a higher form of life—but solely to support their own life and to maintain their own existence. The plant could not continue to exist without the mineral, and the animal could not continue to exist without the plant. These are their chief and indispensable sources of life. And then, when the mineral is incorporated into the structure of the plant, and the plant is incorporated into the organism of the animal, the identity of the mineral and the plant is lost—gone. If anything corresponding to this holds good in the spiritual sphere, then when the Spirit of God seizes hold of the dead soul, that soul ought to lose all individuality, and be incorporated into the Universal Spirit; which in other words is pantheism.

In the three kingdoms of nature—the mineral, the vegetable and the animal— man stands at the head. The two below exist for his use, and his basis is in the mineral. Man's physical organisation is essentially made of the mineral—the dust of the ground. The plant is the intermediary agent through which this is effected. The plant seizes hold of the mineral, not to give the mineral life, but like a hungry man does so merely to satisfy its own wants, and maintain its own existence. No change takes place upon the mineral, further than that its molecular arrangement is altered, and it becomes moulded into a new form. In essence, the mineral is always the same, whether in the body or out of the body.

In the same way the animal acts upon the plant, and in its own complex laboratory moulds that into part of a new and higher organic structure—not by giving it any new kind of life—not by altering its constitution in any way; for its sugar and its starch, its gluten and its minerals, are just the same as ever they were. But they are now arranged into an entirely new form, and made to subserve a new and a higher purpose. Thus, the mineral becomes the plant, and the plant becomes the animal—man lives on both. The origin is the mineral. "Dust thou art, and unto dust thou shalt return." The physical organism is only dust.

But man is more than a mineral or a plant, and he is also more than a mere animal. In so far as his physical organisation is concerned he is merely a higher kind of animal.

But the being created in the image and likeness of God is above and entirely different from all kinds of animals. He has a body, but he is essentially a spiritual being and has an immortal soul.

Revelation teaches, and reason corroborates the fact that man consists of soul, body, and spirit. The visible body is the tabernacle in which he dwells and acts in this visible world. The spiritual part of the man is the intermediate link between the lower creation and God. God speaks to this spiritual being, manifests himself to him, and has communion with him. There is no such intercourse or communion between God and any of the animal creation. This spiritual being can reflect and reason about his origin, and about the constitution of his being. No mere animal can do this. The regenerated man can do more than this—

Realising his true relationship to God as a son to a Father—realising the true end and object of his being—living in God and living to God—he consecrates himself, and the world around him, made for his use, the mineral, the vegetable, and the lower animal, in an organic form, the house he dwells in as a temple for His service; and thus all nature is made to reflect back the glory of God.

THE END.

www.ingramcontent.com/pod-product-compliance
Lightning Source LLC
Chambersburg PA
CBHW030313170426
43202CB00009B/985